Frosting for All Pastries and Cakes Cookbook

Simple Yet Delicious Frosting Recipes for All Cakes and Pastries

BY: GRACE BERRY

License Notes

Table of Contents

Introduction

Do you want to entice your loved ones with new baking creations? This book will improve your cake decorating skills and provide you with some amazing frosting recipes you can make at home. Want to be able to decorate like a professional! Grab your copy and start creating!

Decorating a cake is interesting and exciting. With natural colors, variety of shapes and flavors, every time you frost, it is a creation of art. The recipes we provide will save you money. It will unleash your creativity; ingredients will be quality-controlled, and you will save money. For a family celebration or a Sunday afternoon tea party, this book is perfect for bringing your family together.

There are a story and a purpose to Every frosting!

Pineapple Coconut Frosting

For weekend and holiday guest hosting, treat your visitors to this subtle, tangy vibe.

Serves: 6

Time: 10 mins.

Ingredients:

- Pineapple (2 cups canned crushed, undrained)
- unsalted butter (2 cups, room temperature)
- A pinch salt
- vanilla extract (1 tbsp)
- confectioners' sugar (8 cups)
- meringue powder (2 tbsp)
- coconut flakes (1 tbsp)

Directions:

1. Add the pineapple to a food processor and blend until smooth. Pour the result into a medium saucepan, bring to a boil over medium-high heat and then, simmer until the mixture reduces by two-thirds of a cup. Set aside to cool.

2. In a bowl, beat the butter with a mixer until smooth.

3. Add the salt and vanilla, whisk further until well incorporated.

4. Mix in the sugar 2 cups at a time until the mixture is smooth. Pour in the pineapple and whisk until well combined.

5. Pour in the coconut flakes, fold in with the mixer until adequately distributed.

6. Use the frosting on cakes.

Avocado Dark Chocolate Frosting

Any health freaks out there? This avocado-combo blends excellently and runs smoothly on the tongue!

Serves: 6

Time: 10 mins.

Ingredients:

- butter (1 ½ cups unsalted, room temperature)
- avocado (1 medium soft, pitted and pulp extracted)
- confectioner's sugar (1 ½ cups)
- dark chocolate (1 cup, melted)
- vanilla extract (1 tsp)
- milk (3 tbsp)

Directions:

1. Cream the butter and avocado in a medium bowl over low speed until smooth.

2. Add the sugar 2 tablespoons at a time and continue mixing until smooth.

3. Pour in the dark chocolate, vanilla, milk, and continue whisking until very smooth.

4. Use the frosting on cakes.

Red Buttercream Frosting

Vibrant and attractive! On a platter with different frostings, I bet your curious mind will head for this first. Top this on red velvet cake and make it a wow-some thrill.

Serves: 4

Time: 10 mins.

Ingredients:

- butter (2 cups unsalted, room temperature)
- heavy cream (2 tbsp)
- confectioner's sugar (8 cups)
- salt (½ tsp)
- vanilla extract (1 tbsp)
- food coloring (½ tsp red powder)

Directions:

1. Cream the butter in a medium bowl over low speed.

2. Add the heavy cream and beat until smooth.

3. Whisk in the sugar 1 cup at a time until well combined.

4. Add the salt, vanilla extract, and red food coloring. Mix well until smooth.

5. Use on cakes.

Funfetti Frosting

Hands down for the children! They deserve this any day. I am not sure why adults will splurge on funfetti but catch my husband and me on this sometimes. *embarrassed*

Serves: 6

Time: 10 mins.

Ingredients:

- butter (1 cup, room temperature)
- confectioner's sugar (4 cups)
- vanilla (1 tsp)
- coconut cream (2 tbsp)
- funfetti (2/3 cup)

Directions:

1. In a medium bowl, cream the butter and add the sugar 1 cup at a time while mixing until smooth.

2. Add the vanilla and coconut cream and blend until smooth.

3. Mix in the funfetti until adequately distributed.

4. Use the frosting on cupcakes.

White Chocolate Frosting

White chocolate is an excellent alternative for dark chocolate when you want some variation. Enjoy this frosting on a wide range of cake flavors.

Serves: 6

Time: 10 mins.

Ingredients:

- butter (1 ½ cups unsalted, room temperature)
- confectioner's sugar (1 ½ cups)
- chocolate (1 cup white, melted)
- vanilla extract (1 tsp)
- milk (3 tbsp)

Directions:

1. Cream the butter in a medium bowl over low speed while adding 1 tablespoon of sugar at a time. Keep beating until smooth.

2. Pour in the white chocolate, vanilla, milk, and continue whisking until very smooth.

3. Use the frosting on cakes.

Coffee Buttercream Frosting (Dairy-Free)

Breakfast perfection for board meetings, early morning team meeting, etc. Have them with coffee for a rounded satisfaction.

Serves: 6

Time: 10 mins

Ingredients:

- instant coffee granules (3 tbsp)
- water (1½ tbsp boiling)
- butter (1 cup, room temperature)
- coconut cream (2 tbsp)
- confectioner's sugar (2 cups)
- vanilla extract (¼ tsp)

Directions:

1. In a medium bowl, combine the coffee granules with the boiling water and set aside to cool.

2. Cream the butter and coconut cream in a medium bowl using an electric mixer.

3. Add the sugar ¼ cup at a time until smooth.

4. Mix in the vanilla and coffee mixture until well combined.

5. Use the frosting on cakes.

Peanut Butter Frosting

Nut butter rock in frostings too! I use peanut butter here, but you can play with all sorts of nut butters-my second favorite being almond butter. They work well with mostly vanilla, fruit, and chocolate-flavored cakes.

Serves: 4

Time: 10 mins

Ingredients:

- flour (½ cup, plain)
- peanut butter (1 cup)
- milk (5 tbsp)
- vanilla extract (½ tsp)
- maple syrup (½ cup, sugar-free)

Directions:

1. Add the flour to a medium saucepan and stir-fry until slightly golden.

2. Pour the flour and remaining ingredients into a blender and process until smooth.

3. Use on cakes.

Coconut Chocolate Frosting

I like the Thai flavor that coconut cream gives this chocolate blend. I will top this on coconut cake for a more intense flavor.

Serves: 6

Time: 10 mins.

Ingredients:

- vegan semi-sweet chocolate chips (1 ¼ cup, melted)
- coconut cream (1 cup)

Directions:

1. Freeze an aluminum boil for 1 hour.

2. Add the chocolate to the bowl and cream using an electric mixer.

3. Mix in the coconut cream 2 tablespoons at a time until smooth.

4. Allow sitting for a few minutes to thicken the frost.

5. Use on cakes.

Cream Cheese Frosting

Now, get me on cream cheese any day as a spread on bread, in a stew, and definitely as frosting. I mostly can't get enough and I know you share the same sentiments.

Serves: 4

Time: 10 mins.

Ingredients:

- butter (½ cup unsalted, room temperature)
- cream cheese (8 oz, room temperature)
- confectioner's sugar (4 cups)
- vanilla extract (2 tsp)
- salt (¼ tsp)

Directions:

1. In a medium bowl, beat the butter and cream cheese until well combined.

2. Whisk in the sugar 1 cup at a time until smooth.

3. Add the vanilla, salt, and whisk until adequately combined and the right consistency achieved.

4. Use on cakes.

White Cake Frosting

So pure to devour, but we did in our kitchen! Set this frosting as a base for cake floral décor –an excellent choice for weddings and kid parties.

Serves: 6

Time: 10 mins.

Ingredients:

- butter (1 cup, room temperature)
- vanilla extract (2 tsp)
- salt (1/8 tsp)
- confectioner's sugar (4 cups)
- coconut milk (2 tbsp)

Directions:

1. In a medium bowl, using beaters, whisk the butter, vanilla, and salt until smooth.

2. Gradually, add the sugar (1 cup at a time) and coconut milk (2 teaspoons at a time) while mixing until evenly combined.

3. Use the frosting on cakes.

Mango and White Chocolate Frosting

Subtleness like a Sunday morning and so is the feel, but not the taste. It is striking!

Serves: 6

Time: 15 mins.

Ingredients:

- vegan butter (1 cup, room temperature)
- vegan white chocolate (1 cup, melted)
- mango puree (¾ cup)
- mango extract (1 tsp)
- confectioner's sugar (5 cups)

Directions:

1. In a medium bowl, cream the butter.

2. Add the chocolate and mix until smooth.

3. Mix in the mango puree and mango extract until well combined.

4. Whisk in the sugar 1 cup at a time until well incorporated and your desired consistency achieved.

5. Use on cakes.

Gingerbread Mascarpone Frosting

A way to get into the kids' hearts when there's a ton of chores to get out of the way. They won't hesitate the help for this reward.

Serves: 6

Time: 10 mins.

Ingredients:

- cream cheese (4 oz, room temperature)
- mascarpone cheese (1 ½ cups, room temperature)
- heavy cream (2 tbsp)
- confectioner's sugar (2 cups)
- vanilla extract (½ tsp)
- ginger (1/3 cup minced crystallized)
- salt (¼ tsp)

Directions:

1. In a medium bowl, beat the cream cheese and mascarpone cheese until well combined.

2. Slowly mix in the heavy cream until smooth.

3. Whisk in the sugar 1 cup at a time and vanilla until well blended.

4. Add the ginger, salt, and mix well until adequately combined and the right consistency achieved.

5. Use on cakes and desserts.

Strawberry Chocolate Frosting

Berries and chocolate are always a good idea. Why shouldn't they go together in frosting?

Serves: 4

Time: 10 mins.

Ingredients:

- vegan butter (1 cup, room temperature)
- dark chocolate (1 cup vegan semi-sweet, melted)
- strawberries (¼ cup fresh, pureed)
- vanilla extract (1 tsp)
- confectioner's sugar (5 cups)

Directions:

1. In a medium bowl, cream the butter.

2. Add the chocolate and mix until smooth.

3. Mix in the strawberry puree and vanilla extract until well combined.

4. Whisk in the sugar 1 cup at a time until well incorporated and your desired consistency achieved.

5. Use on cakes.

Minty Frosting

Christmas, peppermint, and pale green set us in the right holiday moods. Don't they? You'll need this one for that vibe.

Serves: 6

Time: 10 mins.

Ingredients:

- butter (2/3 cup unsalted, room temperature)
- milk (¼ cup)
- mint extract (1 tsp)
- green food coloring (4-6 drops)
- confectioner's sugar (6 cups)

Directions:

1. Cream the butter in a medium bowl until smooth.

2. Slowly whisk in the milk until smooth.

3. Mix in the mint extract and green coloring until the mixture is well combined.

4. Whisk in the sugar 1 cup at a time until smooth.

5. Use on cakes.

Lavender Chocolate Frosting

My friend, Summer hooked me up on this lavender love and boy, when I tried it in frosting, I had to share the experience here. While lavender can be overpowering in scent using a little bit in frosting is surprisingly subtle and nourishing.

Serves: 6

Time: 10 mins.

Ingredients:

- coconut cream (½ cup)
- culinary lavender (2 tbsp, dried)
- vegan butter (2 cups, room temperature)
- confectioner's sugar (5 cups)
- cocoa powder (½ cup unsweetened)
- vanilla extract (1 tbsp)

Directions:

1. Pour the coconut cream and lavender into a container, cover, and chill overnight in the refrigerator.

2. The next day, strain the lavender out of the coconut cream and set aside.

3. Cream the vegan butter in a medium bowl using a mixer.

4. Add the confectioner's sugar (1 cup at a time) and cocoa powder (2 tablespoons at a time) while whisking until smooth.

5. Mix in the flavored coconut cream and vanilla until creamy and smooth.

6. Use the frosting on cakes.

Chocolate Butter Frosting

I'll confess I don't like dark chocolate a lot, but chocolate frostings are the only ones that get me eating so much chocolate. This one is creamy; I love it, and I know you'll be crazy about it!

Serves: 6

Time: 10 mins.

Ingredients:

- butter (1½ cups, room temperature)
- cocoa powder (1 cup unsweetened)
- milk (½ cup)
- confectioner's sugar (5 cups)
- vanilla extract (2 tsp)

Directions:

1. Cream the butter and cocoa powder in a medium bowl until smooth.

2. Slowly whisk in the milk (a tablespoon at a time) and sugar (a cup at a time) until smooth.

3. Mix in the vanilla extract until the mixture is well combined and the desired consistency achieved.

4. Use on cakes.

Dark Chocolate Frosting

For the chocolate fanatics, this option is as natural and sharp on color as can get!

Serves: 6

Time: 10 mins.

Ingredients:

- vegan butter (1 ½ cups unsalted, room temperature)
- cofectioner's sugar (1 ½ cups)
- dark chocolate (1 cup vegan, melted)
- vanilla extract (1 tsp)
- coconut milk (3 tbsp)

Directions:

1. Cream the butter in a medium bowl over low speed until smooth.

2. Add the sugar 2 tablespoons at a time and continue mixing until well incorporated.

3. Pour in the dark chocolate, vanilla, coconut milk, and continue whisking until very smooth.

4. Use the frosting on cakes.

Caramel Frosting

Caramel anyone? Yup! Caramel frostings are one of my best enjoyed!

Serves: 6

Time: 10 mins.

Ingredients:

- sugar (1 cup brown)
- milk (¼ cup)
- butter (½ cup, cubed)
- sugar (2 ½ cups confectioner's)

Directions:

1. Heat the brown sugar, milk, and butter in a large saucepan over low heat. Stir continually until the sugar dissolves.

2. Increase the heat to medium but do not stir. Cook until the caramel bubbles and is amber in color.

3. Pour the caramel into a mixer and allow cooling to room temperature.

4. Gradually whisk in the sugar until creamy and well combined.

5. Use on cakes.

Rosette Sugar Frosting

One recommendation for bridal showers and baby girl naming parties. Something about rose inspires this, so I made sure to include some rose flavors.

Serves: 4

Time: 10 mins.

Ingredients:

- butter (½ cup, room temperature)
- shortening (½ cup)
- confectioner's sugar (4 cups)
- culinary rose extract (2 drops)
- vanilla extract (1 tsp)
- cream (3 tbsp whipped)
- food coloring (¼ tsp pink)

Directions:

1. In a medium bowl, cream the butter and shortening using an electric mixer until smooth.

2. Add the sugar a cup at a time while still mixing.

3. Pour in the rose extract, vanilla extract, milk, and mix until evenly combined.

4. Whisk in the food coloring until smoothly combined.

5. Spoon the frosting into a piping bag and swirl on cakes and sugar biscuits.

Greek Yogurt Raspberry Frosting

Rich in tastes and nutrients; have these as a Mediterranean dessert! I don't know why I just know it tastes great!

Serves: 6

Time: 10 mins.

Ingredients:

- raspberries (¼ cup fresh)
- yogurt (2 cups plain Greek)
- vanilla extract (2 tsp)
- sugar (1 cup confectioner's)

Directions:

1. Puree the raspberries in a blender until smooth and pour into a medium bowl.

2. Add the yogurt, vanilla, and sugar. Whisk with a mixer until smooth.

3. Use the frosting on cakes.

Classic Vanilla Frosting

Another easy one that works on every cake type and flavor. You should learn to make this one at your fingertips. Meanwhile, they are always a hit!

Serves: 6

Time: 10 mins.

Ingredients:

- butter (1 ½ cups unsalted, room temperature)
- buttercream (6 tbsp, room temperature)
- vanilla extract (1 tbsp)
- salt (¼ tsp)
- sugar (5 ½ cups confectioners')

Directions:

1. Beat the butter in a medium bowl until smooth.

2. Add the buttercream and whisk until well incorporated.

3. Whisk in the vanilla extract and salt until well combined.

4. Slowly mix in the sugar a cup at a time until the frosting is smooth.

5. Use on cakes.

Pumpkin Cream Frosting

October is for pumpkins, and so are these frostings! Got parties this season? Serve these toppings on cakes, and you will grab in some treats.

Serves: 6

Time: 10 mins

Ingredients:

- butter (1 cup, room temperature)
- pumpkin puree (½ cup)
- confectioner's sugar (4 cups)
- vanilla extract (1 tsp)
- cinnamon powder (¼ tsp)
- nutmeg powder (¼ tsp)
- cream (1 tbsp whipped)

Directions:

1. Cream the butter and pumpkin puree in a medium bowl using an electric mixer until smooth.

2. Add the sugar 1 cup at a time and cream further at low speed.

3. Add the vanilla, cinnamon, nutmeg, and mix further until well combined.

4. Mix in the whipped cream until smooth.

5. Use the frosting on cakes.

Banana Whipped Cream Frosting

Banana frostings are my second favorites after cream cheese. There's something about their sweet-smelling aroma that I can't seem to get enough. I hope you enjoy this too!

Serves: 4

Time: 10 mins

Ingredients:

- banana (1 medium ripe)
- cream (1 ¼ cups whipped)
- confectioner's sugar (1 tbsp)
- vanilla extract (2 tsp)

Directions:

1. Mash the banana in a small bowl using a hand mixer on a low setting until a liquid consistency is achieved.

2. In another bowl, cream the whipped cream, vanilla, and sugar until smooth.

3. Fold in the mashed banana until evenly mixed.

4. Use the frosting on cakes.

Zesty Cream Frosting

An excellent frosting for everyone, especially children. The tang and sweet taste are perfect for lemon or vanilla cupcakes.

Serves: 6

Time: 10 mins.

Ingredients:

- butter (½ cup, room temperature
- cream cheese (8 oz, room temperature)
- lemon (½, zested and juiced)
- sugar (5 cups of confectioner's)

Directions:

1. Beat the butter, cream cheese, lemon zest, and lemon juice in a mixer until well combined.

2. Add and mix in the sugar 1 cup at a time until adequately combined.

3. Use on lemon cakes.

Mango Frosting

With mango in season, this frosting is a wise choice for using up your mangoes before they go bad. Top them on grain-inspired cakes.

Serves: 6

Time: 10 mins.

Ingredients:

- shortening (1 cup)
- butter (½ cup)
- mango puree (¾ cup)
- mango extract (1 tsp)
- sugar (5 cups confectioner's)
- meringue powder (1 tsp)

Directions:

1. Beat the shortening and butter in a medium bowl until smooth.

2. Whisk in the mango puree and extract until well combined.

3. Slowly mix in the sugar and meringue powder a cup at a time until the frosting is smooth.

4. Use on cakes.

One-Minute Chocolate Frosting

Something for the rush and it's chocolate!

Serves: 6

Time: 10 mins.

Ingredients:

- butter (6 tbsp, room temperature)
- salt (pinch)
- water (3 tbsp boiling)
- cocoa powder (½ cup, unsweetened)
- confectioner's sugar (1 ½ cups)

Directions:

1. Cream the butter in a large bowl with a mixer.

2. Add the salt, boiling water, cocoa powder, and mix until smooth.

3. Whisk in the sugar two tablespoons at a time until smooth and your preferred consistency achieved.

4. Use the frosting on cakes.

Strawberry Whipped Cream Frosting

Berries and cream anyone? Every girl's favorite! Of course!

Serves: 6

Time: 10 mins

Ingredients:

- strawberries (¼ cup fresh)
- cream (1 ¼ cups whipped)
- sugar (½ cup confectioner's)
- vanilla extract (2 tsp)

Directions:

1. Add the strawberries in a blender until smooth.

2. Add the whipped cream and whisk until smooth.

3. Mix in the confectioner's sugar and vanilla until well combined.

4. Use the frosting on cakes.

Oreo Frosting

Why can't I get past Oreos on the shelf when grocery shopping? For that reason, I always have enough to work out many decadent recipes. Oreo frostings are one of my favorites for when I grab non-decorated cupcakes from the cake shop. This topping makes dessert all the better!

Serves: 6

Time: 10 mins.

Ingredients:

- butter (2 cups unsalted, room temperature)
- confectioner's sugar (8 cups)
- whipping cream (¼ cup)
- salt (½ tsp)
- Oreos of your flavor choice (1 cup crushed)
- vanilla extract (2 tsp)

Directions:

1. Beat the butter in the bowl on medium speed until smooth.

2. Slowly add in the sugar, 1 cup at a time while alternating with small splashes of whipping cream.

3. Once the frosting is of your desired consistency, mix in the salt and vanilla at low speed.

4. Add the Oreos and continue mixing on low until adequately incorporated.

5. Use on cake or dessert.

Lime Whipped Cream Frosting

Mexican vibes in mind? Alternatively, are you trying to substitute with lime meringue pie without the trouble of baking? Make and use this frosting on store-bought cakes.

Serves: 6

Time: 10 mins.

Ingredients:

- butter (½ cup, room temperature)
- cream (¾ cup whipped)
- lime (1, zested and juiced)
- confectioner's sugar (5 cups)

Directions:

1. Beat the butter, whipped cream, lime zest, and lime juice in a mixer until well combined.

2. Add and mix in the sugar 1 cup at a time until adequately combined.

3. Use on cakes.

White Whipped Cream Frosting

The most basic type of frosting to make! If you've never made any frosting before, you can kick off with this beginner special.

Serves: 6

Time: 1 hr. 15 mins.

Ingredients:

- cream (2 cups heavy whipping)
- sugar (1/3 cup confectioner's)
- chocolate instant pudding mix (½ cup white)

Directions:

1. Freeze an aluminum mixing bowl for 1 hour before making the frost.

2. Take the bowl out and add the whipping cream. Beat using an electric mixer until fluffy.

3. Add the sugar and continue whisking.

4. Just before a stiff peak forms, pour in the pudding mix and whisk until well combined, slightly thickened, and stiff peak forms.

5. Use on cake or dessert.

Conclusion

Thank you so much for sticking with us all the way to the end of the Frosting for All Pastries and Cakes Cookbook. I hope you enjoyed creating all 30 simple yet delicious frosting recipes for all cakes and pastries.

The only way I can continue to provide you with quality content is by understanding how my previous books made you feel. So, please stop by the platform on which you purchased the book to share your thoughts. Until next we meet, keep on cooking.

Cheers!

Author's Afterthoughts

I can't find the perfect words to tell you how grateful I am that you gave this book a chance. I know it must not have been easy seeking this book out and going for it, especially since there are multitudes of materials out there with related content.

You bought the book, but you didn't stop there. You continued, took this journey with me, and read every page back to back. I have to say, you make all this worth it.

I would like to know your thoughts about this book too. Your comments may also help others who are yet to download this book make a decision. What's better than one person reading a book? Two people reading it.

Thank you,

Grace Berry

About the Author

Grace Berry started as a book reviewer after she graduated from college with a degree in creative writing. Afterward, she worked as an editor for a local magazine. She resigned her post and opted to work as a freelance journalist, writing for newspapers and magazines, online and offline.

On one of such assignments, she wrote content for a food blog – a gig she found interesting. Excited about her discovery, she delved deeper into the food world, rediscovering her concept of food. She took a break from freelancing and sought local restaurateurs and chefs out to gather everything she could about their processes and cooking methods; an encounter she documented and wrote about later.

Grace figured out that she could combine her flair for writing with her newfound love for everything food, so she took a plunge and started writing about recipes and other information related to getting the best from the kitchen to the dining.

Now, she has compiled some of her years of research and experiment into a single volume of work, combining storytelling with factual information. Grace hopes to do more, and maybe start a catering business or a restaurant of her own in the future. At the moment, though, recipe developer and cookbook writer will have to do.

Manufactured by Amazon.ca
Bolton, ON